GRAMMAR

Practice Book D

Sentence Expansion • Parts of Speech
Capitalization and Punctuation • Verb Tenses

Authors: Molly Rodgers
           Linda M. Zimmer
Editor: Christine A. Swanson
Art Director: Charles Cary
Illustrator: Anni Matsick

An Essential Learning Product ™

INTRODUCTION

Grammar is the science of language. It is the tool with which students refine and perfect their working knowledge of language. Knowing the basics of grammar allows them to speak and write according to accepted norms. They learn to use words correctly, according to established rules of standard usage. This knowledge can then be applied to all written and spoken communication.

This practice book sharpens students' knowledge of basic grammar skills, such as sentences, nouns, pronouns, verbs, and verb tenses. Higher-level concepts, such as adverbs, adjectives, prepositions, conjunctions, and compound sentences are taught as well. Emphasis is given to combining and expanding sentences, enabling students to think beyond the concept of the simplest sentence construction. Students are encouraged to check written sentences for correct use of various parts of speech. A section on capitalization and punctuation provides rules for the mechanics of writing and practice in applying those rules.

Grammar Practice Book D is intended for use by students at any level above Grade 4. Readability has been carefully controlled for younger students, but the approach and design make the book useful for older, language-delayed students or students who speak English as a second language.

The book may be used in the classroom as a supplement to a basal program. Or it may be used at home by students who need practice. The book is self-paced so that students can use it independently. Answers are provided in the back of the book so students can check their own work.

Pages build confidence through immediate success; the size of the page is "student-friendly," not intimidating. Occasional check-up exercises are provided to remind students to check their work. They have an opportunity to revise their answers before checking the answer page. Helpful hints and clues assist students in completing the page.

Students using the Essential Learning Products *Grammar Practice Books* have the opportunity to gain a practical knowledge of standard speech patterns, increase self-esteem upon successful completion, and improve their performance on the grammar and usage sections of standardized tests.

CONTENTS

SENTENCES

A sentence is a group of words that expresses a *complete thought*. A sentence always begins with a capital letter and has a punctuation mark at the end.
There are four kinds of sentences.

- A *statement* tells something. It ends with a period.
  Photography is my hobby.

- A *question* asks something. It ends with a question mark.

  Where is your camera?

- A *command* makes a request or gives an order. It ends with a period.

  Take a picture of me with my dogs.

- An *exclamation* shows surprise or strong feeling. It ends with an exclamation point.

  What beautiful photographs these are!

After each sentence write **S** for *statement,* **Q** for *question,* **C** for *command,* or **E** for *exclamation.* Write the correct mark at the end of each sentence.

Example: Please bring your camera to the fair. <u> C </u>

1. Who are the people in this picture _____

2. They are a group of jugglers at the fair _____

3. What bright costumes they are wearing _____

4. May I take a picture with your camera _____

5. Show me what to do _____

Check Your Work

Did you remember the four kinds of sentences? Check your answers in back of the book.

☐ Yes   Go on to page 6.
☐ No   Go back to page 4 and check again.

SENTENCES

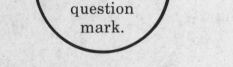

A question asks something and ends with a question mark.

Change each statement to a question.

Example: Yolanda is taking a karate class.

Is Yolanda taking a karate class?

1. The class has already started.

_____

2. The students are using tumbling mats.

_____

3. They will learn to fall safely.

_____

4. Karate is good exercise.

_____

A sentence *fragment* is an incomplete sentence. It does not express a complete thought.

traveled to South Dakota last year

You can correct sentence fragments by adding words to express a complete thought.

The Fergusons traveled to South Dakota last year.

Write **S** if the group of words is a sentence. Write **F** if it is a fragment.

Example: Stopped at a famous national monument. _F_

1. Mount Rushmore a huge granite cliff. ____

2. Faces are carved into the cliff. ____

3. The faces of four American presidents. ____

4. The monument fourteen years to complete. ____

5. What other things in South Dakota? ____

7

Rewrite the fragments from page 7 as complete sentences. Add words to make complete thoughts.

Example: Stopped at a famous national monument. __F__

The family stopped at a famous national monument.

_____

_____

_____

_____

_____

_____

A noun names a *person, place, thing,* or *idea.* A *common* noun names any person, place, thing, or idea. A *proper* noun names a particular person or place and begins with a capital letter.

Look at these examples of nouns. Notice that the proper nouns begin with capital letters.

People: judge, leaders, Kristen, Mrs. Wagg

Places: subway, stadium, Ohio, Houston

Things: saddle, frog, telephone, canoe

Ideas: encouragement, generosity, liberty, fury

A noun that names one is a *singular* noun. A noun that names more than one is a *plural* noun. Most plural nouns end in *s* or *es.*

| one whale | three whales |
| a stitch | ten stitches |

Circle the nouns.

inventor   habit   direct   satisfy   hamsters   Scott   pleasure   shovel

lagoon   inner   frozen   England   pearl   rainbow   settlers   after

A proper noun names a particular person or place and
begins with a capital letter.

Write a proper noun to go with each common noun.

Example: city _Boston_

1. state _____

2. dog _____

3. president _____

4. country _____

5. store _____

6. man _____

7. teacher _____

8. singer _____

After each noun in the sentence write whether it is common or proper. Then write whether it is singular or plural.

Example: Mrs. Kaufman assigned reports on ancient civilizations.

Mrs. Kaufman,   proper,   singular

reports,   common,   plural

civilizations,   common,   plural

1. Ted gave a report on ancient Egypt.

_____

2. Most Egyptians lived near the Nile River.

_____

Check Your Work	Did you remember the difference between common and proper nouns? Did you remember the difference between singular and plural nouns? Check your answers in the back of the book.
	☐ Yes Go on to page 12.
	☐ No Go back to page 9 and check again.

To form the plural of most nouns you add *s*.

    skater → skater*s*   adventure → adventure*s*.

Add *es* to nouns that end in *s, ss, ch, sh, x,* or *z*.

    radish → radishes   address → addresses

    mass → masses   fox → foxes

A plural noun names more than one.

For nouns that end in a consonant plus *y*, change the *y* to *i* before adding *es*.

    ferry → ferries   daisy → daisies

If a noun ends in a vowel plus *y*, just add *s*.

    turkey → turkeys   tray → trays

Write the plural of each noun.

1. argument _____

2. baby _____

3. brush _____

4. lady _____

5. monkey _____

6. tax _____

7. ash _____

8. porcupine _____

9. mess _____

10. mammal _____

11. Sunday _____

12. society _____

Check Your Work

Did you remember how to form plurals of nouns? Check your answers in the back of the book.

☐ Yes   Go on to page 14.
☐ No   Go back to page 12 and check again.

Some nouns form their plurals in unusual ways.

child→children   woman→women

man→men   mouse→mice

Some nouns have the same plural form as the singular form.

deer→deer   fish→fish

Form the plural of most nouns by adding *s*.

For some nouns that end in *f* or *fe*, change the *f* to *v* before adding *es* or *s*.

loaf→loaves   knife→knives   wife→wives

But remember, if a noun ends in *ff*, just add *s*.

cliff→cliffs   cuff→cuffs

Write the plural of each noun.

1. calf _____

2. man _____

3. shelf _____

4. goldfish _____

5. puff _____

6. woman _____

7. reindeer _____

8. elf _____

9. grandchild _____

10. life _____

11. leaf _____

12. staff _____

Check
Your
Work

Did you remember how to form unusual plurals? Check
your answers in the back of the book.

☐ Yes Go on to page 16.
☐ No   Go back to page 14 and check again.

Nouns that show ownership, or possession, are called *possessive* nouns.

Form possessive nouns by adding an apostrophe (') and the letter *s* to singular nouns.

Matt + *'s* = Matt*'s*   announcer + *'s* = announcer*'s*

horse + *'s* = horse*'s*   Mr. Cross + *'s* = Mr. Cross*'s*

Form the possessive of plural nouns by adding an apostrophe after the final *s*.

racers + (') = racers'   bosses + (') = bosses'

the Hendersons + (') = the Hendersons'

For plural nouns that do not end in *s*, add an apostrophe and the letter *s*.

men + *'s* = men's   children + *'s* = children's

Write each phrase with a possessive noun.

Example: the boots of my sister *my sister's boots*

1. the car of the Fosters _____

2. the hair of Phyllis _____

3. the voices of the women _____

4. the eyes of two deer _____

5. the bicycle of Patrick _____

6. the tails of roosters _____

Check Your Work

Did you remember how to form possessive nouns? Check your answers in the back of the book.

☐ Yes Go on to page 18.
☐ No Go back to page 16 and check again.

17

VERBS

A verb shows *action* or *being*.

An action verb shows physical or mental action.

> The band *marched* across the field. (physical action)

> We *admired* their new uniforms. (mental action)

A *linking* verb shows being. It links two parts of a sentence.

> That drummer *is* my sister.

In this sentence the verb *is* is a linking verb. It shows that one thing in the sentence (drummer) is the same as another (sister).

The verb *be* and its forms are the most common linking verbs. Other linking verbs are *seem, become, feel, grow, remain, appear, look,* and *stay.*

> She *becomes* nervous before each game.

In this sentence *becomes* is a linking verb connecting *she* and *nervous.*

Circle the verb in each sentence. Write **A** if it is an action verb and **L** if it is a linking verb.

1. A band practices for many hours. _____

2. The musicians are excellent performers. _____

3. They become more skilled with practice. _____

4. The conductor leads them in each song. _____

5. They follow his movements carefully. _____

6. The band members appear confident. _____

7. This song is the audience's favorite. _____

8. Everyone applauds at the end. _____

9. We talked about the concert on the way home. _____

An action verb shows physical or mental action.

A linking verb shows being.

19

Verbs can show actions that take place at different times.

Present tense verbs show action that is happening now.

> The Statue of Liberty *welcomes* people
>
> to New York Harbor.

Past tense verbs show action that took place some time before now. Form the past tense of most verbs by adding *ed* to the present tense.

> It *arrived* as a gift from France in 1885.

Future tense verbs show action that will take place some time after now. Form the future tense by placing the word *will* before the present tense form of a verb.

> It *will stand* for many years as a
>
> symbol of freedom.

This is how a verb is written in the past, present, and future tenses. Notice the verb endings and the word *will*. Many verbs form their past and future tenses this way.

Present Tense	Past Tense	Future Tense
I arrive	I arrived	I will arrive
you arrive	you arrived	you will arrive
he, she, it arrives	he, she, it arrived	he, she, it will arrive
we arrive	we arrived	we will arrive
you arrive	you arrived	you will arrive
they arrive	they arrived	they will arrive

21

Spelling Hint: When a verb ends in *e*, drop final *e* before adding *ed*.

Write these verbs in the past tense.

I approach _____   we imagine _____

you deliver _____   he designs _____

they divide _____   it weighs _____

Write these verbs in the future tense.

I purchase _____   you state _____

they lift _____   it sails _____

we stop _____   she waves _____

Present tense verbs show action happening now.

Past tense verbs show action that happened.

Future tense verbs show action that will happen.

Underline the correct verb tense to complete each sentence.

1. In 1990 America (celebrated, will celebrate) Earth Day.

2. People (learn, learned) about the environment.

3. We (will need, need) clean air and water.

4. Even today poisons (pollute, polluted) the air.

5. We now (realize, will realize) the dangers.

6. Throughout the next century citizens (will work, worked) for a cleaner earth.

The verb *be* has unusual forms.

Present Tense		**Past Tense**		**Future Tense**	
I am	we are	I was	we were	I will be	we will be
you are	you are	you were	you were	you will be	you will be
he, she, it is	they are	he, she, it was	they were	he, she, it will be	they will be

Write a form of *be* to complete each sentence.

1. (past) The rain _____ steady last night.

2. (past) The dogs _____ not afraid of the thunder.

3. (present) They _____ very brave during storms.

4. (present) I _____ quite proud of them.

5. (future) One day I _____ a dog trainer.

6. (future) Then other dogs _____ as good as mine.

24

Have is another unusual verb.

Present Tense		Past Tense		Future Tense	
I have	we have	I had	we had	I will have	we will have
you have	you have	you had	you had	you will have	you will have
he, she, it has	they have	he, she, it had	they had	he, she, it will have	they will have

Write a form of *have* to complete each sentence.

1. (present) The American flag _____ fifty stars.

2. (past) At one time it _____ only thirteen.

3. (past) The country _____ only thirteen states.

4. (present) Now we _____ fifty states.

5. (future) Possibly the flag _____ more stars one day.

6. (future) Maybe we _____ more than fifty states in the U.S. someday.

25

VERBS

Do is another unusual verb.

Present Tense		**Past Tense**		**Future Tense**	
I do	we do	I did	we did	I will do	we will do
you do	you do	you did	you did	you will do	you will do
he, she, it does	they do	he, she, it did	they did	he, she, it will do	they will do

Write a form of *do* to complete each sentence.

1. (future) Mindy _____ a favor for me.

2. (present) We _____ our chores together.

3. (past) Yesterday I _____ her jobs.

4. (future) Today she _____ the dishes for me.

5. (present) Frank _____ them on Sundays.

6. (past) Last week he _____ his homework with Mindy.

26

Here are some other verbs that have unusual forms.

Present Tense	Past Tense	Present Tense	Past Tense
begin	began	know	knew
break	broke	make	made
bring	brought	run	ran
come	came	say	said
eat	ate	take	took
find	found	teach	taught
give	gave	think	thought
go	went	write	wrote

The future tense of these verbs is formed by placing the word *will* in front of the present tense verb.

Examples: I will go, you will bring, they will find

we will come, she will run, you will think

VERBS

Complete the chart.

Present	Past	Future
1. we come	_____	_____
2. _____	he brought	_____
3. _____	_____	they will say
4. you take	_____	_____
5. _____	I ran	_____
6. _____	_____	it will go
7. she thinks	_____	_____
8. _____	_____	I will know
9. _____	he began	_____

Circle the correct verb to complete each sentence.

1. I (thinked, thought) about my favorite movie.

2. Everyone (said, sayed) they liked it.

3. A visitor (comed, came) from Mars on a flying saucer.

4. He (bringed, brought) offers of friendship.

5. Some people (ran, runned) away from from their homes.

6. Others (knowed, knew) they would be safe.

7. One girl (beginned, began) talking with the visitor.

8. Soon people from both planets (maked, made) friends.

9. They (wrote, writed) each other letters.

10. Some Martians (taught, teached) the earth people their language.

11. Some earth people (goed, went) to visit their new friends.

29

VERBS

Write each sentence in the past tense.

1. Carlotta finds a pen pal in Australia.

_____

2. They begin their friendship through a club.

_____

3. They write each other many letters.

_____

Check Your Work

Did you remember how to form the past tense of unusual verbs? Check your answers in the back of the book.

☐ Yes Go on to page 31.
☐ No   Go back to page 27 and check again.

When you write a verb and the word *not,* you can write a shorter version called a *contraction.* When you write a verb contraction, write the two words together, with no space between. Then remove the **o** from the word *not,* and write an apostrophe (') in its place.

Here are some common verb contractions.

did + not = didn't

does + not = doesn't

do + not = don't

has + not = hasn't

is + not = isn't

was + not = wasn't

were + not = weren't

would + not = wouldn't

could + not = couldn't

should + not = shouldn't

have + not = haven't

had + not = hadn't

are + not = aren't

will + not = won't

Notice that the verb contraction *won't* is unusual.

will + not = won't

The verb contraction for *can* + *not* can be written two ways: *cannot* or *can't.*

VERBS

Write each sentence so it means the *opposite*. Use a verb contraction.

Example: Karim could reach the top shelf.

Karim couldn't reach the top shelf.

1. He can see the box of pencils.

_____

2. Janis is ready for the exam.

_____

3. She was in the library all morning.

_____

Check Your Work	Did you remember how to form verb contractions? Check your answers in the back of the book. ☐ Yes Go on to page 33. ☐ No Go back to page 31 and check again.

The subject is the naming part of a sentence. It tells who or what the sentence is about. It can be one word or several words.

> *Flames* leaped into the air.
>
> *The forest ranger in the tower* had spotted a fire.

Circle the subject in each sentence.

1. Forest fires destroy trees and animals.

2. Fires have many causes.

3. Careless people may start fires accidentally.

4. Lightning sometimes strikes the trees.

5. Damage from forest fires can spread for miles.

6. Teams of fire fighters keep the fire under control.

SUBJECTS AND PREDICATES

A sentence may have two subjects. When a sentence has two subjects, it is called a *compound subject*. The parts of a compound subject are joined by the word *and* or *or*.

Food and *drinks* are served on airplanes.

Milk or *juice* comes with your breakfast.

Circle the compound subject in each sentence below. Draw a box around the word that joins the two parts.

Example: (The pilots) [and] (flight attendants) make the passengers comfortable.

1. Parents and children often fly together.

2. Luggage and pets fly in a special section.

3. Small suitcases or packages may be carried on the plane.

4. The passengers and flight crew eat their meals in the air.

5. A cook and kitchen workers prepare the meals on the ground.

6. A magazine or a movie makes a long flight enjoyable.

Add the words in parentheses to each subject to make a compound subject. Write the sentences.

Example: Diane flew to Florida. (Glen)

Diane and Glen flew to Florida.

1. The pilot took them on a tour of the plane. (the co-pilot)

_____

_____

Use *and* or *or* to join the parts of a compound subject.

2. Their tickets are in this envelope. (their money)

_____

3. Sandwiches were served during the flight. (tacos)

_____

4. Carmen met them at the airport. (his father)

_____

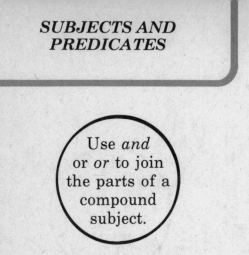

Use *and* or *or* to join the parts of a compound subject.

Expand each sentence.

Turn the subject into a compound subject.

Example: Pancakes are my favorite breakfast.

Pancakes and waffles are my favorite

breakfast.

1. Blueberries taste great in pancakes.

_____

_____

2. The plates are on the table.

_____

_____

The *predicate* of a sentence is the part that tells about the subject. The predicate can be one word or several words. It always contains a verb or a verb phrase.

Reminder: A verb phrase has a helping verb and a main verb.

A gray dolphin *leaped out of the water*.
The audience in the marine park *applauded*.
The trainer *was smiling*.

The verb in the predicate must agree with the subject of the sentence. That means that when the verb is in the present tense, you need to add an *s* if the *subject* is singular.

Singular subject: A dolphin communicates through different sounds.

Plural subject: Dolphins communicate through different sounds.

37

Underline the predicate in each sentence.
Then circle the verb in each predicate.

A verb shows action or being.

1. Archaeologists study the ruins of ancient cultures.

2. The ruins reveal facts about the people of the past.

3. The archaeologist works with a team.

4. The team digs through the earth carefully.

5. Some of the items are fragile.

6. Careless diggers could break them.

7. Scientists prepare the objects for museums.

Circle the correct verb to complete each sentence.

1. Each year the fifth-graders (goes, (go)) on a field trip.

2. This year the trip (are, is) to a science museum.

3. It (contain, contains) a huge model of the human heart.

4. Visitors (walks, walk) through the heart.

5. The heartbeat (echoes, echo) all around them.

6. Another exhibit (explain, explains) the sense of smell.

7. We (sniff, sniffs) things without seeing them.

A singular subject must have a singular verb.

Check Your Work	Did you remember how to make a subject and a verb agree? Check your answers in the back of the book.
	☐ Yes Go on to page 40.
	☐ No Go back to page 37 and check again.

SUBJECTS AND PREDICATES

A predicate that has two or more verbs is a *compound* predicate. The verbs in a compound predicate are joined by the words *and* or *or*.

> Museums preserve ancient treasures *and* display them.

If there are more than two verbs, write a comma to separate them. This is called a *series*.

> Many visitors view, study, and discuss the precious items.

A sentence may have both a compound subject and a compound predicate.

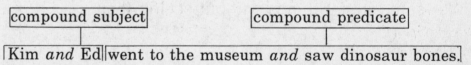

compound subject   compound predicate

Kim *and* Ed went to the museum *and* saw dinosaur bones.

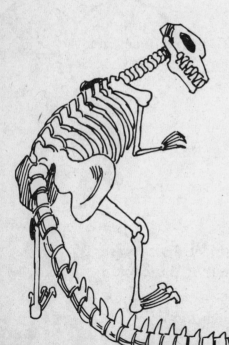

Underline the predicate in each sentence. Check YES if it is a compound predicate. Check NO if it is not a compound predicate.

Compound Predicate?

	YES	NO
1. The old car coughed and sputtered.	☐	☐
2. Mrs. Hanley turned right and headed toward the city.	☐	☐
3. She passed many skyscrapers.	☐	☐
4. Traffic slowed down and crept along.	☐	☐
5. Horns were honking everywhere.	☐	☐

Check Your Work

Did you remember how to recognize a compound predicate? Check your answers in the back of the book.
☐ Yes   Go on to page 42.
☐ No   Review page 40 and check again.

Combine each pair of sentences. Write sentences with compound predicates. Use the words *and* or *or* to join the verbs.

Example: Robins fly south in winter. Robins return in the spring.

_____*Robins fly south in winter and return in the spring.*_____

1. The mother robin builds the nest. The mother robin feeds the young birds.

_____

_____

2. People hear the robin's song. People think of spring.

_____

_____

3. Bird watchers study birds. Bird watchers take pictures of them.

_____

Expand each sentence. Add the words in parentheses to make a compound predicate.

Example: Rubber keeps out water. (stretches into different shapes)

_____*Rubber keeps out water and stretches into different shapes.*_____

1. Rubber shoe soles last a long time. (are quiet)

_____

_____

2. People depend on rubber products every day. (use them)

_____

_____

3. Students write with pencils. (use rubber erasers)

_____

_____

DIRECT OBJECTS

A *direct object* receives the action of the verb.
It tells you *what* or *whom* after the verb.

Joshua lifted the rock. He found a snake. He told Ben.

The words *rock, snake,* and *Ben* tell you what or who
was *lifted, found,* and *told.* They receive the action of the
verbs. They are the direct objects of the verbs.

To find the direct object, you must find the verb first.
Then say the verb and ask *what?* or *whom?*

Joshua lifted the rock.   He told Ben.

   (lifted what?)   (told whom?)

Draw one line under the verb.
Draw two lines under the direct object.

1. I bought some seeds.

2. I planted a garden.

3. My brother helped me.

4. We are growing tomatoes.

5. A garden requires hard work.

6. I pull the weeds.

7. I water the plants.

8. I will make a big salad.

9. I will choose a yummy dressing.

DIRECT OBJECTS

Find the direct objects in each sentence.
Write the word in the blank.

1. Dad is making dinner. _____

2. We ordered tacos. _____

3. I cut some lettuce. _____

4. Tommy grated the cheese. _____

5. Dad cooks the beef. _____

6. We called Alison. _____

7. She was riding her bike outside. _____

8. Alison will wash the dishes after dinner. _____

Add a direct object to
complete each sentence.

1. The city is building _____ .

2. Five different bulders drew _____ .

3. The mayor chose _____ .

4. People can see _____ .

5. The bulldozers are digging _____ .

6. For the walls the builder will use _____ .

7. Next month they will open _____ .

8. The building will contain _____ .

47

DIRECT OBJECTS

Write your own sentences with direct objects. Use the verbs below, and add your own nouns as direct objects.

bring   write   meet   introduce

see   find   admire   practice

1. _____

2. _____

3. _____

4. _____

5. _____

6. _____

7. _____

8. _____

When you write a sentence, the order in which you put the words is important. Usually sentences follow the order of noun-verb. When a verb has a direct object, then the sentence follows the order noun-verb-noun. The direct object comes after the verb. If the words are in the wrong order, the sentence may not make sense. Which sentence do you think follows the correct word order?

Beth bought a hamster.   A hamster bought Beth.

Rearrange each group of words to make a logical sentence.

1. Beth the hamster put in a cage.

_____

2. all animals likes she.

_____

3. a dog also she has.

_____

DIRECT OBJECTS

Remember that a direct object answers the question *what?* or *whom?* after the verb. These sentences do not have direct objects.

The moving van was parked in the driveway.

The horn blared loudly.

Read each sentence below. Check whether the sentence has a direct object or not.

	Direct Object	No Direct Object
1. We are moving to Utah.	☐	☐
2. The movers packed the boxes.	☐	☐
3. They loaded the furniture on the truck.	☐	☐

Check Your Work

Did you remember how to find the direct object? Check your answers in the back of the book.

☐ Yes   Go on to page 51.
☐ No   Go back to page 44 and check again.

An *indirect object* comes before the direct object. It tells *to whom* or *for whom* something was done.

Mr. Laverty gave *Joan* tennis lessons.

In this sentence, the direct object is *tennis lessons*. It receives the action of the verb *gave*. The indirect object, *Joan,* tells to whom Mr. Laverty gave the lessons. You could write the sentence this way:

Mr. Laverty gave tennis lessons *to Joan*.

An indirect object can be a noun or a pronoun.

noun

Joan asked her *teacher* many questions.

pronoun

He showed *her* the secrets of winning.

These are the pronouns that can be used as indirect objects.

me   you   him   her   it   us   them

Here are some verbs that take indirect objects.

give   tell   buy   ask   show
offer   teach   write   make   find

51

An indirect object tells *to whom* or *for whom* an action was done.

Circle the indirect object in each sentence.

1. Bicycles offer people cheap transportation.

2. Owning a bike gives young people freedom.

3. It also teaches them responsibility.

4. I offer my brother my bike quite often.

5. My parents will buy him his own bike this year.

6. I will find him an old horn in the garage.

7. Dad gave me that horn for my first bike.

8. He also made me this rack for a water bottle.

9. Dad will take us biking next month.

Circle the indirect object in each sentence.

1. Last year Officer Stark taught the children the safety rules of riding.

2. He showed Jenny the proper place for lights.

3. She asked him lots of questions.

4. He got her a special book on bicycle safety.

5. A biker should always give drivers a hand signal.

6. Signals tell other people a biker's intentions.

7. Reflectors give you an advantage at night.

8. The lights show others your location on the road.

9. Jenny's parents bought her a bike helmet.

INDIRECT OBJECTS

Write each sentence. Replace the underlined words with an indirect object.

Example: Can I give some good news <u>to you</u>?

Can I give you some good news?

1. Mrs. Tremain sent two concert tickets <u>to us</u>.

_____

2. She bought a ticket <u>for Carolyn</u>, too.

_____

3. We can give <u>to you</u> a ride to the concert.

_____

Check Your Work

Did you remember how to use a direct object in a sentence? Check your answers in the back of the book.

☐ Yes   Go on to page 55.
☐ No   Go back to page 51 and check again.

Write five sentences of your own with indirect objects.
Use these verbs.

gave   told   offered   wrote   made

1. _____

_____

2. _____

_____

3. _____

_____

4. _____

_____

5. _____

_____

PRONOUNS

A *pronoun* replaces a noun. You can use pronouns as *subjects, direct objects,* or *indirect objects.*

Subject Pronouns						**Object Pronouns**				

Singular: I you he she it   Singular: me you him her it
Plural: we you they   Plural: us you them

The noun that a pronoun replaces is called its *antecedent.* A pronoun must agree with its antecedent. That means if the antecedent is singular, the pronoun must be singular. If the noun names a man or boy, use *he* or *him.* If the noun names a woman or girl, use *she* or *her.*

Bud said he would come over tonight.

In this sentence *Bud* is the antecedent. The pronoun *he* agrees with *Bud* because it is singular and names a man or boy. The antecedent may not be in the same sentence with the pronoun. It may be in the sentence that came before.

Bud is late. He is usually on time.

Change the underlined nouns in each sentence to a
pronoun. Write the pronoun in the space.

Example: June said <u>June</u> has a new hobby. *she*

1. June is collecting photographs of <u>her friends</u>. _____

2. My favorite is the photo of <u>Henry</u>. _____

3. He is sitting on a fence with <u>Judy</u>. _____

4. <u>Judy</u> is wearing a straw hat. _____

5. <u>The hat</u> is too big for Judy. _____

6. Her face is hidden under <u>the hat</u>. _____

7. <u>Henry and Judy</u> look so funny. _____

8. Can I show this picture to <u>Henry and Judy</u>? _____

Use *I, you, he, she, it, we, they* as subjects.

Use *me, you, him, her, it, us, them,* as objects.

57

PRONOUNS

Draw an arrow from each pronoun to its antecedent.

Example: Marco told the class about a book he read.

> **Hint:** The antecedent may be a word in the sentence before.

1. The book was interesting. It was a biography of Mark Twain.

2. Twain worked on the Mississippi when he was a young man.

3. Marco said he learned about Mark Twain's sense of humor.

4. One funny book is about a frog. It was a champion jumper.

5. The frog's owner lost a bet he made with a stranger.

6. Twain loved the Mississippi River. He wrote wonderful stories about it.

7. Marco has a favorite story. It is *The Prince and the Pauper*.

58

Circle the correct pronoun to complete each sentence.

1. The television is a great invention. (It, He) teaches and entertains people.

2. Some programs win awards because (we, they) investigate important problems.

3. Television reporters give the day's news. (You, They) talk to experts and witnesses.

4. That woman reports on money matters. (She, It) gives good advice on making a budget.

5. Some reporters stand in front of the White House when (we, they) report from Washington.

Check Your Work

Did you remember how to choose pronouns that agree with their antecedents? Check you answers in the back of the book.

☐ Yes Go on to page 60.
☐ No   Go back to page 56 and check again.

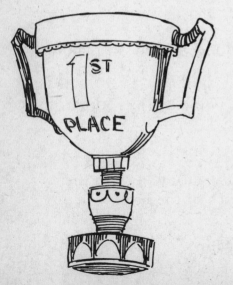

A possessive pronoun shows ownership. These are the possessive pronouns.

Singular: my, mine, your, yours, his, her, hers, its

Plural: our, ours, your, yours, their, theirs

Use *my, your, his, her,* and *its* with nouns.

> This is *your* trophy.
>
> Are those *my* medals?
>
> Which is *his* locker?

Use *mine, yours, his, hers, ours,* and *theirs* alone.

> This trophy is *yours.*
>
> Are those medals *mine?*
>
> Which locker is *his?*

Possessive pronouns must agree with their antecedents.

> Teri wore the ribbon on *her* jacket.

Write each sentence. Replace each underlined noun with a possessive pronoun.

Example: Atlanta is <u>Wendy's</u> favorite city.

Atlanta is her favorite city.

1. She once visited <u>Mr. Hart's</u> family there.

_____

2. <u>His parents'</u> house is just outside the city.

_____

Rewrite this sentence, using possessive pronouns. Write the sentence two different ways.

Example: This book belongs to Alice.

This is her book. This book is hers.

3. This party is for you.

_____

_____

PRONOUNS

The subject pronouns are *I, you, he she, it, we, they*.

When you use pronouns as part of a compound subject, remember to use the subject pronouns. When you talk about yourself as part of a compound subject, remember to put the word *I* last.

> Bettina and *I* did a report about the moon.

> *She and I* visited the library last week.

To test whether you should use a subject pronoun, say or write the sentence without the other person's name.

> Bettina and I did a report about the moon.

You would not say, "*Me* did a report about the moon." So you know you should use the pronoun *I*.

When you use pairs of pronouns as direct or indirect objects, remember to use object pronouns.

> The teacher gave *Hal and her* an extra day.

Use the same test to see whether you are using the correct pronoun. Take out the other person's name and say or write the sentence. You would not say, "The teacher gave *she* another day," so you know that *her* is correct.

Expand each sentence by adding a pronoun to the subject, direct object, or indirect object. The underlined words show where to add the pronoun.

Example: <u>Alicia</u> accepted the gift gladly.

Alicia and he accepted the gift gladly.

1. Show <u>the girls</u> your gift.

2. Everyone watched <u>Sandy</u> on the stage.

3. <u>He</u> made a speech about the science fair.

4. <u>Your friends</u> should come to the fair.

PRONOUNS

Circle the correct pronoun or pair of pronouns to complete each sentence.

1. Mr. Cliff hired Jeffrey and (I, me) last summer.

2. I met Mr. Cliff's wife and (he, him) at a softball game.

3. (Him and her, He and she) needed garden helpers.

4. (Jeffrey and I, Me and Jeffrey) mow the lawn every week.

5. Jeffrey has known my sister and (I, me) for a year.

6. (Her and me, She and I) are his two best friends.

Check Your Work

Did you remember which pronouns to use as subjects and objects? Check your answers in the back of the book.

☐ Yes   Go on to page 65.
☐ No   Go back to page 62 and check again.

A conjunction joins words or groups of words. The conjunctions *and, but, or, so, yet, for,* and *nor* join words that have the same function in a sentence. For example, they can join a noun with another noun, a verb with another verb, a phrase with another phrase, and so on.

Thomas Edison invented the phonograph *and* the electric light

He invented *or* improved over a thousand inventions.

He sometimes failed *but* never became discouraged.

Remember to use a comma when you join more than two words or groups of words.

Some more of Edison's inventions were the stock ticker, the electric pen, and talking motion pictures.

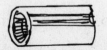

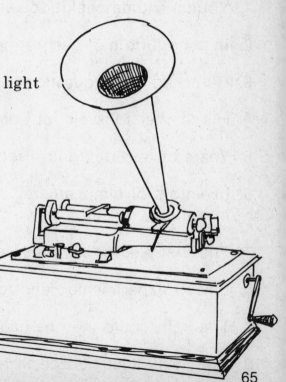

CONJUNCTIONS

Circle the conjunction in each sentence. Underline the words or groups of words each conjunction joins.

Example: As a child Edison lived in <u>Ohio</u> (and) <u>Michigan</u>.

1. Young Thomas held jobs as a newsboy and a telegrapher.

2. In school he had been bright yet unsuccessful.

3. He asked many questions and annoyed the teacher.

4. His mother took him out of school and taught him herself.

5. Years of research and discovery went into the invention of movies.

6. Inventors of film, cameras, lights, and microphones contributed to the invention.

7. The first electric light worked well but burned out quickly.

8. Edison experimented and found a better wire for the light.

9. The light could then be used in homes and offices.

10. During his lifetime Edison received many honors and awards.

Write the conjunction *and, but,* or *or* to complete
each sentence.

1. Would you rather have baked _____ mashed potatoes?

2. Marlene cooked the potatoes, added milk, _____ mashed them.

3. I invited the Andersons to dinner, _____ they could not come.

4. The salt _____ pepper are on the table.

5. Does everyone have a cup _____ a saucer?

6. The peaches are ripe _____ not soft.

7. Please sit here _____ over there.

8. Ray, Donna, _____ Sara will sit in this chair.

9. Did you buy _____ make this bread?

10. David, Karen, _____ Mark all liked the chicken.

67

CONJUNCTIONS

Expand each sentence by adding a conjunction and additional words.

Example: Gwen sent letters to all her friends.

Gwen sent letters and cards to all her friends.

1. I must tell you about my trip to the mountains.

_____

_____

2. I saw deer in the fields every morning.

_____

_____

3. Some wild turkeys flew out of the trees.

_____

_____

A sentence that has one subject and one predicate is a *simple* sentence. A compound sentence is two or more simple sentences joined together.

Cathy never invented anything, but she enjoys books about inventors.

To make this compound sentence, two simple sentences were joined together. Notice that each sentence has a subject and predicate.

Cathy never invented anything.

She enjoys books about inventors.

Use the conjunctions *and, or, but,* or *nor* to join the simple sentences. Write a comma before the conjunction.

A sentence has a subject and a predicate.

Read each sentence. Write **S** if it is a simple sentence.
Write **C** if it is a compound sentence.

1. Whitcomb Judson invented the zipper in 1893. _____

2. He invented it as a fastener for shoes, but it was also used for clothing. _____

3. Zippers soon replaced most buttons and hooks. _____

4. The zipper is a wonderful invention, and we cannot imagine life without it. _____

5. The umbrella is another really useful invention. _____

6. Six inventors worked together on it, and they shared the profits. _____

Check
Your
Work

Did you remember the difference between a simple
sentence and a compound sentence? Check your answers
in the back of the book.

☐ Yes   Go on to page 71.
☐ No   Go back to page 69 and check again.

In each compound sentence underline the two simple sentences.
Circle the conjunction.

Example: <u>Vanilla beans grow on vines,</u> (and) <u>they give flavor to many foods.</u>

1. Cooks can use pure vanilla, or they can buy an imitation.

2. The imitation is cheaper, but it does not taste as good.

3. I like vanilla yogurt, but my favorite flavor is lemon.

4. Yogurt is made from milk, and it has many of the same vitamins.

5. Dad bought me a yogurt machine, and now I make my own yogurt.

Check Your Work	Did you remember which conjunctions are used to join the parts of a compound sentence? Check your answers in the back of the book. ☐ Yes Go on to page 72. ☐ No Go back to page 69 and check again.

COMPOUND SENTENCES

When you join two simple sentences to form a compound sentence, use both a comma and a conjunction.

Sharon loves music, and her parents often take her to concerts.

Each sentence below is incorrect. Rewrite the sentences, adding commas or conjunctions where they are needed.

1. The concert is starting, people are still looking for their seats.

_____

_____

2. They could ask an usher, she would show them the right row.

_____

_____

3. The musicians have tuned their instruments and the conductor is walking to the stand.

_____

_____

Combine these pairs of sentences to make compound sentences. Write the sentences.

Example: Alaska has a cold climate. In some parts the temperatures become quite warm.

Alaska has a cold climate, but in some parts the temperatures become quite warm.

1. Alaska has a large mainland. It includes many islands as well.

_____

_____

2. Fishing is a major industry. Much of the world's salmon comes from Alaska.

_____

_____

3. Anchorage is the largest city. Juneau is the state capital.

_____

_____

COMPOUND SENTENCES

Add a conjunction and another simple sentence to each sentence below to make a compound sentence. Write your compound sentences.

Example: Children all around the world play in Little League.

Children all around the world play in Little League, and its World Series is held every year in Pennsylvania.

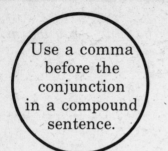
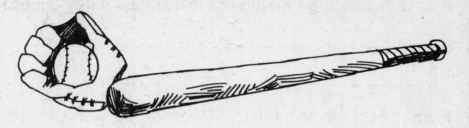

1. Teams must be very good.

_____

_____

2. The players meet people from different countries.

_____

_____

74

Write five compound sentences of your own. Be sure to
use commas and conjunctions.

1. _____

   _____

2. _____

   _____

3. _____

   _____

4. _____

   _____

5. _____

   _____

Adjectives modify nouns or pronouns. Adjectives answer these questions:

What kind?   *yellow* bird, *old* barn, *huge* truck, *ugly* hat

How many?   *one* day, *many* friends

How much?   *more* milk, *less* time

Which one?   *that* house, *those* trees

Like nouns, there are common adjectives and proper adjectives. Proper adjectives should be capitalized.

Asian countries   German cars   Hawaiian islands

Underline the common adjectives and proper adjectives in the sentences.

1. The neighbors had an unusual picnic.

2. There were Swedish meatballs and plain American hamburgers.

3. Everyone brought a different food.

4. The Satos made Chinese egg rolls.

5. My grandparents made a big pot of Hungarian stew.

6. Forty people were invited.

7. Mr. Rodriguez brought spicy chili.

8. Cold Italian ices were the dessert.

9. Everyone had a great time.

Adjectives tell *what kind, how many, how much,* or *which one.*

77

ADJECTIVES

The words *the, a, an* are adjectives called *articles*.
The is a definite article. *A* and *an* are *indefinite* articles.

The book indicates a specific book.

A book indicates any book. It is not specific.

Underline the adjectives, including the articles, in each sentence.

1. The American flag has fifty stars and thirteen stripes.

2. The white stars are set on a blue background.

3. Many different flags appeared in the 1700s.

4. One flag had a rattlesnake on it.

5. A plain red flag had a green tree.

6. One troop of soldiers carried a yellow flag with an elaborate crest on it.

Use one of the adjectives below to complete each sentence.

flat	two	scary	brave
new	weird	brown	leafy
three	many	horrible	

1. Joey had a _____ tent.

2. Joey hiked into the woods with _____ friends.

3. _____ sandwiches and _____ canteens filled their backpacks.

4. They found a _____ spot for the tent.

5. The boys told _____ stories about _____ monsters.

6. Suddenly they heard _____ sounds.

7. One _____ boy peeked out.

8. A _____ owl was sitting on a _____ branch.

79

ADJECTIVES

Imagine how you would describe things to someone who does not know you. Use adjectives in sentences to describe each of these things:

1. the weather today

_____

_____

2. your best friend

_____

_____

3. your room

_____

_____

Adverbs modify, or describe, verbs, adjectives, or other adverbs. They tell *how, when, where, how often,* or *to what extent.*

Adverbs modify verbs:

The author wrote *quickly.*   (wrote how)

The author wrote *yesterday.*   (wrote when)

The author wrote *here.*   (wrote where)

Adverbs modify adjectives:

The book is *so* funny.   (funny to what extent)

It is *fairly* easy.   (how easy)

Adverbs modify other adverbs:

He ran *way* ahead.   (ahead where)

He stopped *quite* suddenly.   (how suddenly)

Notice that an adverb usually comes before the adjective or adverb it modifies. An adverb that modifies a verb may come before the verb, after the verb, or may be apart from the verb.

Often she laughed.   She often laughed.   She laughed often.

Many adverbs are formed by adding *ly* to adjectives.

   complete—completely   sharp—sharply   easy—easily

ADVERBS

Underline the adverb in each sentence, and write whether it tells *how, when, where, how frequently,* or *to what extent*. Draw an arrow from each adverb to the word it modifies.

Example: Have you <u>ever</u> heard of the blues? *when*

1. Bessie Smith was a very fine singer. _____

2. Her family was extremely poor. _____

3. She traveled everywhere to sing. _____

4. She sang the blues so well. _____

5. Her voice was truly rich. _____

6. She never used a microphone. _____

7. Her records became quite popular. _____

8. Audiences always loved her songs. _____

Write one or more of these adverbs to complete each sentence.

easily	far	very	soon	always	early

1. Speaking a foreign language is a _____ valuable skill.

2. We can _____ communicate with people from other countries.

3. People _____ like to hear their own language

   when they are _____ from home.

4. Young people can begin learning other languages _____ in their lives.

5. _____ they can speak and understand a second language.

ADVERBS

Write an adverb to complete each sentence.

Example: The audience sat ___*quietly.*___ (how)

1. The conductor tapped the baton _____ . (how)

2. The musicians looked _____ . (where)

3. The conductor _____ (when) paused _____ . (to what extent)

4. The violins began _____ . (how)

5. _____ (when) the flutes joined _____ . (where)

6. _____ (when) the horns sounded _____ . (where)

7. All the different instruments blended _____
   (to what extent) _____ . (how)

84

Expand each sentence by adding one or more adverbs.
Write the sentences.

Example: Justin sat on the bench.

Justin sat very quietly on the bench.

1. He was hoping for a chance to play.

_____

2. His team needed him.

_____

3. Justin's cast had come off.

_____

4. His broken foot was healed.

_____

ADVERBS

The word *not* is a negative adverb. It usually modifies a verb. When you use the word *not* in a sentence, do not use other negative words, such as *never, nobody, nothing, none, no one, neither, nowhere.*

Incorrect: Vanessa did not see nobody in the yard.
(The incorrect sentence has two negative words—*not* and *nobody*.)

Correct: Vanessa did *not* see *anybody* in the yard.
or
Vanessa saw *nobody* in the yard.

Each incorrect sentence below has two negative words. Write each sentence correctly.

1. Mom did not say nothing about her plans.

_____

2. She was not usually late neither.

_____

3. Luckily Vanessa didn't never forget her key.

_____

Sometimes the words *good* and *well* cause confusion. Remember that *good* is an adjective and *well* is an adverb.

> Bonnie did a *good* job on the scenery for the play.
>
> She draws and paints *well*.

Write *good* or *well* to complete each sentence.

1. The actors learned their parts _____ .

2. Marcie has a _____ role this year.

3. This song would be _____ for the beginning of the play.

4. Marcie sings _____, and she knows the song.

5. The chorus had a _____ practice this morning.

6. Now we need a _____ piano player.

7. Bert reads music _____ .

8. Take a _____ look at this song, Bert.

PREPOSITIONS

A *preposition* is a word that relates a noun or pronoun to another word in the sentence.

The people *in* the picture were smiling.

In this sentence the preposition is *in*. It shows the relationship between *people* and the *picture*.

Here are some common prepositions.

about	as	beyond	from	onto	to
above	at	but	in	out	toward
across	before	by	into	over	under
after	behind	despite	like	past	until
against	below	down	near	since	up
along	beneath	during	of	through	upon
among	beside	except	off	throughout	with
around	between	for	on	till	without

The words that follow a preposition are a *prepositional phrase*. A prepositional phrase begins with a preposition and ends with a noun or pronoun. The noun or pronoun in the prepositional phrase is called the *object of the preposition*.

```
    ┌─────────────────────┐
    │ prepositional phrase │
    └─────────────────────┘
                  │
               object
                  │
The team with the blue jerseys is winning.
```

Remember to use an object pronoun when the object of the preposition is a pronoun.

The quarterback passed the ball *to him*.

PREPOSITIONS

In each prepositional phrase, circle the preposition, and underline the object of the preposition.

1. (through) the open <u>window</u>

2. of a very long speech

3. during class

4. to a tropical island

5. with a frightened crash

6. in Africa

7. for us

8. without any furniture

9. about a wonderful vacation

10. behind the green plaid sofa

11. at home

12. into your bag

13. with me

14. on the beach

15. among my friends

16. under his blue coat

17. toward the dark woods

18. near them

19. beside the car

20. by the bench

Underline the prepositional phrase in each sentence.
Circle each preposition, and draw an arrow to the object
of the preposition.

Example: James is reading a book (about) the stars.

1. Sometimes groups of stars make a picture.

2. These pictures in the sky are constellations.

3. Draw lines between the brightest stars.

4. With a little effort you will see the picture.

5. People have watched stars since ancient times.

6. They invented stories about them.

**Check
Your
Work**

Did you remember which words are prepositions? Check
your answers in the back of the book.

☐ Yes Go on to page 92.
☐ No   Go back to page 88 and check again.

PREPOSITIONS

A preposition shows the relationship between two words in a sentence.

Write a preposition to complete each sentence.

1. An old lamp stood _____ the oak table.

2. _____ the bookcase stood a stack of books.

3. Martha looked _____ the fireplace.

4. She had arrived _____ the others.

5. James was always _____ her.

6. A tall man waited _____ the den.

7. Now a car was driving _____ the driveway.

8. Martha quickly put the paper _____ the fireplace

Add a prepositional phrase to each sentence.
Write the sentence.

Example: Gina found an old photograph album.

> *Gina found an old photograph album in*
> *her grandfather's attic.*

1. She recognized a picture.

_____

_____

2. Uncle Jim took the picture.

_____

_____

3. Her grandfather's house looked different.

_____

_____

CAPITALIZATION AND PUNCTUATION

Write a period at the end of a statement or a command.

> The rain has started again. Take your umbrella.

Write an exclamation point at the end of an exclamation, and a question mark at the end of a question.

> What a nasty day this is!

> When will it stop?

Write the correct mark at the end of each sentence.

1. A hurricane is coming this way tomorrow

2. How should we get ready for it

3. Cover your windows with boards

4. How powerful a hurricane must be

5. It can damage buildings and cars

6. Listen to the radio for instructions

Write initials with capital letters, and write a period after each initial.

      Raymond A. Martin   R. A. Martin

Begin abbreviations of titles with a capital letter. Write a period at the end.

Mr.   Mrs.   Dr.   Ms.   Rev.

Begin abbreviations of proper nouns with a capital letter, and write a period at the end.

Examples:

Days	Saturday—Sat.	Monday—Mon.	Wednesday—Wed.
Months	March—Mar.	August—Aug.	September—Sept.
Streets	Street—St.	Avenue—Ave.	Lane—La.

Abbreviations of common nouns do not begin with capital letters. Some end with periods, and some do not.

quart—qt   foot—ft   inch—in.
pound—lb   mile—mi   minute—min

Do not use periods after metric abbreviations.

millimeter—mm   centimeter—cm   meter—m

Write the abbreviation for each word.

1. Thursday _____

2. Avenue _____

3. Mister _____

4. pound _____

5. Drive _____

6. Sunday _____

7. December _____

8. mile _____

9. centimeter _____

10. April _____

11. Doctor _____

12. inch _____

Check Your Work

Did you remember when to use capital letters and periods? Check your answers in the back of the book.

☐ Yes Go on to page 97.
☐ No   Go back to page 95 and check again.

Write a comma between the name of a city and a state.

Bozeman, Montana   or   Bozeman, MT

Do not use periods after two-letter abbreviations of states.

Florida—FL   Texas—TX   Indiana—IN

Write a comma between the day and year in a date.

July 30, 1992   November 29, 1979

Write a comma after the greeting of a letter.

    Dear Grandma Early,

Circle the item in each row that is written correctly.

1. Tucson, AZ   Tucson AZ,   Tucson AZ

2. Dear Bill   Dear, Bill   Dear Bill,

3. Atlanta Georgia   Atlanta. Georgia   Atlanta, Georgia

4. Dear Uncle Walter,   Dear Uncle, Walter   Dear Uncle Walter

5. July 9, 1987   July, 9 1987   July 9 1987

97

Write a comma to separate two or more words in a series.

George, Donna, Jim, and Teri came for dinner.

They had chicken, peas, and potatoes.

Write a comma after words that introduce a sentence.

First, let me tell you about my day.

Actually, I don't know what happened.

Write a comma to set off the name of a person being spoken to or addressed.

Maureen, your sister is here.

Please come in, Joyce.

Oh, Michael, you can't be serious.

Write commas where they belong in these sentences.

1. Jim how many people went to the show?

2. Well I didn't count them.

3. I saw Brian Lisa Pamela and Tim.

A *quotation* is the exact words a person says or writes. Write quotation marks (" ") around a quotation. A comma sets off the quotation from the rest of the sentence.

> Mrs. Hess said, "Turn right at the corner."

> "Turn right at the corner," said Mrs. Hess.

Notice that in the second sentence Mrs. Hess's words are followed by a comma instead of a period.

Periods, exclamation points, and question marks go inside the quotation marks.

> Bob exclaimed, "What a beautiful view!"

> "What a beautiful view!" Bob exclaimed.

> Mina asked, "Should we take pictures?"

> "Should we take pictures?" Mina asked.

You can break up a long quotation.

> "The road to the old stone quarry," Mrs. Hess said, "is two miles long and runs along the river."

Write each sentence as a quotation. You may place the person's words at the beginning or at the end of the sentence.

Example: Dr. Burrett said that the dog needs a shot.

Dr. Burrett said, "The dog needs a shot."

or

"The dog needs a shot," said Dr. Burrett.

1. Robert replied that Buster had shots last year.

_____

2. The nurse exclaimed that Buster is such a good dog.

_____

3. Sheri said that she loved all animals.

_____

4. Dr. Burrett said that Sheri should become a vet.

_____

Write commas and quotation marks where they belong in each sentence.

1. What is the largest mammal? asked Mrs. George.

2. Miko said It must be the whale.

3. The biggest whale is the blue whale he continued and it is almost 100 feet long.

4. How heavy it must be! exclaimed Sheila.

5. He replied It can weigh as much as 150 tons.

Check Your Work	Did you remember where to put commas, quotation marks, and end marks in quotations? Check your answers in the back of the book.
	☐ Yes Go on to page 102.
	☐ No Go back to page 99 and check again.

Write a capital letter for the word *I*.

I found a wallet on the sidewalk.

Dad and *I* took it to the police station.

Write capital letters to begin proper nouns and proper adjectives.

Sandra Thompson   Luis Vacaro

French bread   Japanese camera

Always begin the first word of a sentence with a capital letter.

*S*ome pictures were inside the wallet.

*G*ive me your name and address.

*C*an you find the owner of this wallet?

*H*ow happy he will be!

102

Cross out the incorrect letters in each sentence. Write capital letters in their place.

       H   R   A

Example: H̶ave you heard of R̶oald A̶mundsen?

1. he was a heroic explorer from norway.

2. he found a sailing route from the atlantic ocean
   to the pacific ocean.

3. It is called the northwest passage.

4. amundsen later took a trip to the antarctic.

5. his group wanted to locate the south pole.

6. i read about his exploration across antarctica.

7. his group of explorers reached their goal in december of 1911.

8. there they set up the norwegian flag.

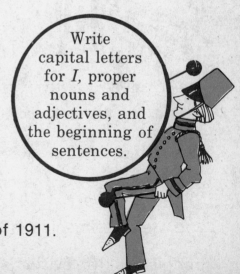

Write capital letters for *I*, proper nouns and adjectives, and the beginning of sentences.

103

CAPITALIZATION AND PUNCTUATION

Use capital letters for the first word and all important words in the titles of books, movies, poems, and magazine articles.

> Gordon read the poem "Casey at the Bat."

Names of books, magazines, newspapers, plays, movies, and television shows should be underlined.

> <u>The Wonder Years</u> is a funny TV show.

Names of stories, poems, magazine articles, book chapters, and songs should be written in quotation marks.

> "Jingle Bells" is one of my favorite songs.

Write each title correctly.

Example: the dream keeper (poem) *"The Dream Keeper"*

1. all summer in a day (story) _____

2. the black pearl (book) _____

3. you are my sunshine (song) _____

4. fraggle rock (television show) _____

Use an apostrophe for possessive nouns.

Singular: Harry's desk   the judge's robe
Plural: the artists' displays   elephants' trunks

Use an apostrophe in contractions.

it's   didn't   wouldn't   wasn't   can't
won't   I'm   you're   we've   he'd

Write apostrophes where they belong in these sentences.

1. Did you hear the two boys idea about buried treasure?

2. Its the craziest idea Ive ever heard.

3. Theyre digging up the Wilsons back yard.

4. Maybe theyll find something, but it wont be treasure.

5. Mr. Wilsons dog buried its bones there.

6. Old dog bones arent worth very much.

7. Wouldnt it be funny if they really found something?

Possessive nouns show ownership.

A contraction is a short way of writing two words.

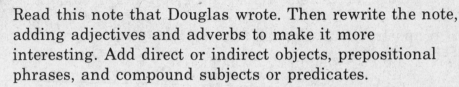

Read this note that Douglas wrote. Then rewrite the note, adding adjectives and adverbs to make it more interesting. Add direct or indirect objects, prepositional phrases, and compound subjects or predicates.

The house has a room with a hidden door. Which room is it? You must figure it out for yourself. Find the door. It will lead to a room. A creature lives there. Do not be afraid. Be sure to bring cookies. The creature likes them. The creature might show you its collection of junk.

Example: *The scary old house has a room near the kitchen with a carefully hidden door.*

Rewrite Douglas's note here.

_____

_____

_____

_____

_____

_____

_____

_____

_____

WRITING A NOTE

Now write a note of your own about any topic you choose. Use compound subjects or predicates, compound sentences, adjectives, adverbs, and prepositional phrases. Enjoy your writing.

Answers

Page 5
1. (?) Q   2. (.) S   3. (!) E   4. (?) Q   5. (.) C

Page 6
1. Has the class already started?
2. Are the students using tumbling mats?
3. Will they learn to fall safely?
4. Is karate good exercise?

Page 7
1. F   2. S   3. F   4. F   5. F

Page 10
Inventor   habit   hamsters   Scott
pleasure   shovel

lagoon   England   Pearl   rainbow
settlers

Page 11
1. Ted, proper, singular
   report, common, singular
   Egypt, proper, singular

2. Egyptians, proper, plural
   Nile River, proper, singular

Page 13
1. arguments   5. monkeys   9. messes
2. babies   6. taxes   10. mammals
3. brushes   7. ashes   11. Sundays
4. ladies   8. porcupines   12. societies

Page 15
1. calves   4. goldfish
2. men   5. puffs
3. shelves   6. women

Page 17
7. reindeer   10. lives
8. elves   11. leaves
9. grandchildren   12. staffs

Page 17
1. the Fosters' car   4. two deer's eyes
2. Phyllis's hair   5. Patrick's bicycle
3. the women's voices   6. roosters' tails

Page 19
1. practices (A)   2. are (L)   3. become
(L)   4. leads (A)   5. follow (A)   6. appear
(L)   7. is (L)   8. applauds (A)   9. talked(A)

Page 22
I approached   we imagined
you delivered   he designed
they divided   it weighed

I will purchase   you will state
they will lift   it will sail
we will stop   she will wave

Page 23
1. celebrated   2. learned   3. need
4. pollute   5. realize   6. will work

Page 24
1. was   2. were   3. are   4. am
5. will be   6. will be

Page 25
1. has   2. had   3. had   4. have
5. will have   6. will have

Page 26
1. will do   2. do   3. did
4. will do   5. does   6. did

Page 28
1. we come   we came   we will come
2. he brings   he brought   he will bring
3. they say   they said   they will say

4. you take   you took   you will take
5. I run   I ran   I will run
6. it goes   it went   it will go

7. she thinks   she thought   she will think
8. I know   I knew   I will know
9. he begins   he began   he will begin

Page 29
1. thought   2. said   3. came   4. brought
5. ran   6. knew   7. began   8. made
9. wrote   10. taught   11. went

Page 30
1. Carlotta found a pen pal in Australia.
2. They began their friendship through a
   club.
3. They wrote each other many letters.

Page 32
1. He can't see the box of pencils.
2. Janis isn't ready for the exam.
3. She wasn't in the library all morning.

Page 33
1. Forest fires   2. Fires   3. Careless
people   4. Lightning   5. Damage from
forest fires   6. Teams of fire fighters

Page 34
1. Parents and children   2. Luggage and pets
3. Small suitcases or packages   4. The
passengers and flight crew   5. A cook and
kitchen workers   6. A magazine or a movie

Page 35
1. The pilot and the co-pilot took them on
   a tour of the plane.
2. Their tickets and their money are in this
   envelope.

3. Sandwiches and tacos were served during the flight. *or* Sandwiches or tacos were served during the flight.
4. Carmen and his father met them at the airport. *or* Carmen or his father met them at the airport.

Page 38
1. (study) the ruins of ancient cultures
2. (reveal) facts about the people of the past
3. (works) with a team
4. (digs) through the earth carefully
5. (are) fragile
6. (could break) them
7. (prepare) the objects for museums

Page 39
1. go 2. is 3. contains
4. walk 5. echoes 6. explains
7. sniff

Page 41
1. coughed and sputtered (YES)
2. turned right and headed toward the city (YES)
3. passed many skyscrapers (NO)
4. slowed down and crept along (YES)
5. were honking everywhere (NO)

Page 42
1. The mother robin builds the nest and feeds the young birds.
2. People hear the robin's song and think of spring.
3. Bird watchers study birds and take pictures of them.

Page 43
1. Rubber shoe soles last a long time and

are quiet.
2. People depend on rubber products and use them every day.
3. Students write with pencils and use rubber erasers.

Page 45.
1. I bought some seeds.
2. I planted a garden.
3. My brother helped me.
4. We are growing tomatoes.
5. A garden requires hard work.
6. I pull the weeds.
7. I water the plants.
8. I will make a big salad.
9. I will choose a yummy dressing.

Page 46.
1. dinner 2. tacos 3. lettuce
4. cheese 5. beef 6. Alison
7. bike 8. dishes

Page 49
1. Beth put the hamster in a cage.
2. She likes all animals.
3. She also has a dog.

Page 50
1. no direct object 2. direct object
3. direct object

Page 52
1. people 2. people 3. them
4. brother 5. him 6. him
7. me 8. me 9. us

Page 53
1. children 2. Jenny 3. him

4. her 5. drivers 6. people
7. you 8. others 9. her

Page 54
1. Mrs. Tremain sent us two concert tickets.
2. She bought Carolyn a ticket, too.
3. We can give you a ride to the concert

Page 57
1. them 2. him 3. her 4. She 5. It
6. it 7. They 8. them

Page 58
1. book It
2. Twain he
3. Marco he
4. book It
5. owner he
6. Twain He, Mississippi River it
7. story It

Page 59
1. It 2. they 3. They 4. She 5. the

Page 61
1. She once visited his family there.
2. Their house is just outside the city.
3. This is your party. This party is yours

Page 64
1. me 2. him 3. He and she
4. Jeffrey and I 5. me 6. She and I

Page 66
1. a newsboy (and) a telegrapher
2. bright (yet) unsuccessful
3. asked many questions (and) annoyed the teacher

4. took him out of school (and) taught him herself.
5. research (and) discovery
6. film, cameras, lights, (and) microphones
7. worked well (but) burned out quickly
8. experimented (and) found a better wire for the light
9. homes (and) offices
10. honors (and) awards.

Page 67
1. or 2. and 3. but 4. and 5. and
6. but 7. or 8. or 9. or 10. and

Page 70
1. S 2. C 3. S 4. C
5. S 6. C

Page 71
1. Cooks can use pure vanilla, (or) they can buy an imitation.
2. The imitation is cheaper, (but) it does not taste as good.
3. I like vanilla yogurt, (but) my favorite flavor is lemon.
4. Yogurt is made from milk, (and) it has many of the same vitamins.
5. Dad bought me a yogurt machine, (and) now I make my own yogurt.

Page 72
1. The concert is starting, but people are still looking for their seats.
2. They could ask an usher, and she would show them the right row.
3. The musicians have tuned their instruments, and the conductor is

walking to the stand.

Page 73
1. Alaska has a large mainland, and it includes many islands as well.
2. Fishing is a major industry, and much of the world's salmon comes from Alaska.
3. Anchorage is the largest city, but Juneau is the state capital.

Page 77
1. unusual 2. Swedish, plain, American
3. different 4. Chinese, egg 5. big, Hungarian 6. Forty 7. spicy 8. cold, Italian 9. great

Page 78
1. The American flag has fifty stars and thirteen stripes.
2. The white stars are set on a blue background.
3. Many different flags appeared in the 1700s.
4. One flag had a rattlesnake on it.
5. A plain red flag had a green tree.
6. One troop of soldiers carried a yellow flag with an elaborate crest on it.

Page 79
Possible answers:
1. new 2. two 3. Many, three 4. flat
5. weird, scary 6. horrible 7. brave
8. brown, leafy

Page 82
1. Bessie Smith was a very fine singer. (to what extent)
2. Her family was extremely poor. (to what extent)

3. She traveled everywhere to sing. (where)
4. She sang the blues so well. (to what extent, how)
5. Her voice was truly rich. (to what extent)
6. She never used a microphone. (when)
7. Her records became quite popular. (to what extent)
8. Audiences always loved her songs. (when)

Page 83
1. very 2. easily 3. always, far 4. early 5. Soon

Page 86
1. Mom did not say anything about her plans. *or* Mom said nothing about her plans.
2. She was not usually late either.
3. Luckily Vanessa didn't ever forget her key. *or* Luckily Vanessa never forgot her key.

Page 87
1. well 2. good 3. good 4. well
5. good 6. good 7. well 8. good

Page 90
1. (through) window
2. (of) speech
3. (during) class
4. (to) island
5. (with) crash
6. (in) Africa
7. (for) us
8. (without) furniture
9. (about) vacation
10. (behind) sofa
11. (at) home
12. (into) bag
13. (with) me
14. (on) beach
15. (among) friends
16. (under) coat
17. (toward) woods
18. (near) them
19. (beside) car
20. (by) bench

Page 91
1. (of) stars
2. (in the sky)
3. (between) the brightest stars
4. (With) a little effort
5. (since) ancient times
6. (about them)

Page 94
1. (.) 2. (?) 3. (.) 4. (!) 5. (.) 6. (.)

Page 96
1. Thurs.	5. Dr.	9. cm
2. Ave.	6. Sun.	10. Apr.
3. Mr.	7. Dec.	11. Dr.
4. lb	8. mi	12. in.

Page 97
1. Tucson, AZ 2. Dear Bill, 3. Atlanta,
Georgia 4. Dear Uncle Walter,
5. July 9, 1987

Page 98
1. Jim, how many people went to the show?
2. Well, I didn't count them.
3. I saw Brian, Lisa, Pamela, and Tim.

Page 100
1. Robert replied, "Buster had shots last year." *or*
   "Buster had shots last year," Robert replied.
2. The nurse exclaimed, "Buster is such a good dog!" *or*
   "Buster is such a good dog!" exclaimed the nurse.

3. Sheri said, "I love all animals." *or*
   "I love all animals," said Sheri.
4. Dr. Burrett said, "Sheri (You) should become a vet." *or*
   "Sheri (You) should become a vet," Dr. Burrett said.

Page 101
1. "What is the largest mammal?" asked Mrs. George.
2. Miko said, "It must be the whale."
3. "The biggest whale is the blue whale," he continued, "and it is almost 100 feet long."
4. "How heavy it must be!" exclaimed Sheila.
5. He replied, "It can weigh as much as 150 tons."

Page 103
1. He, Norway 2. He, Atlantic Ocean, Pacific Ocean 3. It, Northwest Passage 4. Amundsen, Antarctic 5. His, South Pole 6. I, Antarctica 7. His, December 8. There, Norwegian

Page 104
1. "All Summer in a Day"
2. The Black Pearl
3. "You Are My Sunshine"
4. Fraggle Rock

Page 105
1. boys' 2. It's, I've 3. They're, Wilsons' 4. they'll, won't 5. Mr. Wilson's 6. aren't 7. Wouldn't

112